CONTENTS

Bakery Basics

Read these tips to help you set up your work station and craft using the tools and materials in this book.

♥ PREP WORK

- Before you start crafting, cover your work surface with a sheet of wax paper or foil.
- Keep toothpicks and a damp paper towel handy. True pastry chefs never know when they may be creating a mini messy masterpiece.

♥ AIR-DRY CLAY

- Most projects will firm up in 30 minutes. However, it's best to wait overnight for the clay to fully dry before you let other people hold them.
- Keep the clay in an air-tight storage baggie after you open it. It will dry up if left out too long.
- If you forget to put the clay away, add a small amount of water to it. Massage and squeeze the wet clay until it feels soft again.
- You can make any of the recipes in this book with air-dry clay from your local arts-and-craft store.
- Smoosh the clay to make it softer. Let the clay rest for a few minutes to make the clay harder.

♥ GLAZE

- Use the glaze any time you want the clay to look shiny or to glue something to the clay.
- Remember to put the glaze cap back on the bottle so that the glaze doesn't dry up.
- After using the glaze a couple times, you may want to wipe the brush with a damp paper towel. This way you will get a smooth coat every time.
- If you get any glaze on your hands or work surface, simply wash it off with warm soapy water.

Remember,
wash your hands after crafting.

These projects are super cute, but they are not toys. Keep finished projects and crafting supplies away from babies and pets.

The supplies are perfect for crafting, but make sure to keep them away from real food and baking supplies.

Don't eat a mini baked good even if it looks sweet. It is NOT food.

MAKE A BALL

To make a big ball of clay, tear off a bit about the size you want it to be. Roll the clay between your palms in a circular motion until it's nice and round.

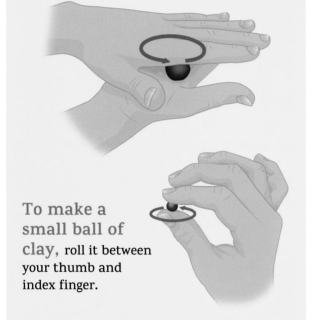

To make a small ball of clay, roll it between your thumb and index finger.

MEASURING CLAY

At the begining of each project, there is a chart that shows how many balls of clay and how big each ball should be.

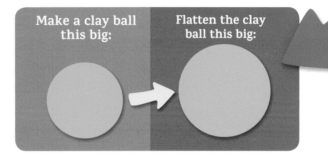

Make a clay ball this big:	Flatten the clay ball this big:

After you've rolled each ball, sit it on top of the chart to make sure you've got the right size. Don't roll inside the book because the clay may stick to the pages.

- If the ball is too small, add a bit of clay and roll the ball until it's smooth.
- If the ball is too big, pinch off a bit of clay and roll it again. Remember to put your scraps back into an air-tight baggie to use later!

USING THE BAKERY TOOL

Use this end to add a mouth and texture.

Use this end to cut the clay.

Use this tool to roll the clay flat.

Donut

HERE'S THE SWEETEST WAY TO START YOUR DAY.

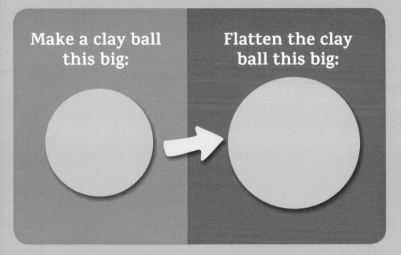

Make a clay ball this big:

Flatten the clay ball this big:

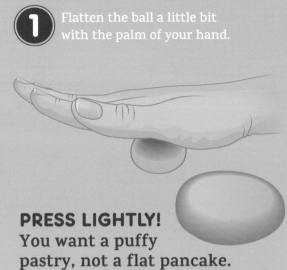

1 Flatten the ball a little bit with the palm of your hand.

PRESS LIGHTLY!
You want a puffy pastry, not a flat pancake.

MAKE A DONUT HOLE

USE THIS END OF THE TOOL:

2 Poke the tool all the way through the center of the donut, until its tip touches your work surface.

3 Pick up the donut and keep twisting the tool around (like a drill) until you've reached the smooth neck of the tool.

Once there is a hole, twist the tool around a few times to smooth the hole.

4 Tear off any extra clay that may be stuck to the tool's tip or the bottom of the donut. Then pull the tool out by twisting the tool the same way out the top.

If you want to add a face, skip ahead to page 11.

Decorate

HOW TO Ice

DONUT ICING

Make a clay ball this big:

Flatten to this size:

1 To make icing, squish the clay ball super flat with your finger. Keep pressing until you have a nice round-ish shape.

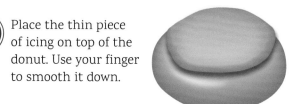

If your flattened frosting sticks to the work surface, use the tool like a spatula to gently scoop it off.

USE THIS END OF THE TOOL:

2 Place the thin piece of icing on top of the donut. Use your finger to smooth it down.

3 Use the tool to push the icing into the donut hole. Use your finger again to smooth it down.

4 Paint glaze on the icing to make it look even yummier! The glaze makes the clay shiny.

MAKE A COIL

Lay a ball on your work surface and use your pointer finger to roll it back and forth. The ball will turn into a rope.

To make the same thickness from end to end, use even pressure and roll your fingers over different parts of the tube as it gets longer.

You can make a coil any size so it can be used for all types of decorations. **GET CREATIVE!**

HOW TO Drizzle

ICING DRIZZLE

Make a clay ball this size:

Make a coil this long:

1 Roll a thin coil out of a clay color that pops against the pastry's icing.

2 Zig-zag the thin coil over an iced donut. Tear off the extra clay drizzle if it's too long.

The more you stretch it, the more real it looks.

3 Use the tool or your finger to press the drizzle into the hole.

4 Paint glaze on the icing drizzle to make it look like real icing or drizzled chocolate.

HOW TO SPRINKLE

Make sure to have a scrap piece of paper or wax paper under the donut so you don't get sprinkles everywhere!

1 Paint glaze wherever you want mini beads or glitter to stick.

2 Shower with sweetness!

Make this recipe with white tissue from home.

Coconut

1 Make a donut with white icing.

2 Cut very thin strips of white facial tissue or gift wrap tissue paper.

3 Paint glaze on the white icing and generously sprinkle pieces of tissue on top. Use a toothpick to stick them down.

Add this faux coconut to cupcakes and cakes!

Make a Face

When you've finished decorating, decide where to add a face.

1 Use this end of the tool to make a mouth.

It's easiest to make the mouth first, so you can use it as a guide to line up the eyes and cheeks.

SWEET TREAT

Hold the tool like this to make a smile.

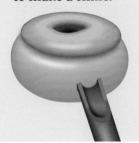

POUTY PASTRY

Hold the tool like this to make a frown.

2 To add a pair of eyes, use two dabs of glaze on either side of the mouth. Then stick the flat side of the bead eyes to the glaze dots.

To make a chocolate pastry's peepers pop, add two tiny balls of white clay where the eyes should go. Then place the bead eyes on top.

3 To add cheeks, use two dabs of glaze under the eyes. Then stick on sequin cheeks to the glaze dots.

Use the glaze to add paper punch-outs.

SEQUIN TIP:
Dip the tip of a toothpick in glaze to make a great sequin picker-upper tool.

11

MILK'S LIFE PARTNER!

Cookie

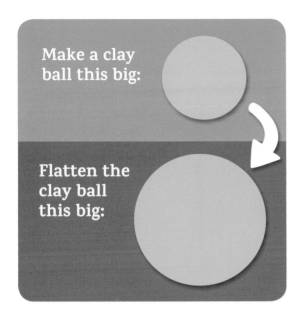

Make a clay ball this big:

Flatten the clay ball this big:

① Flatten the ball with the palm of your hand.

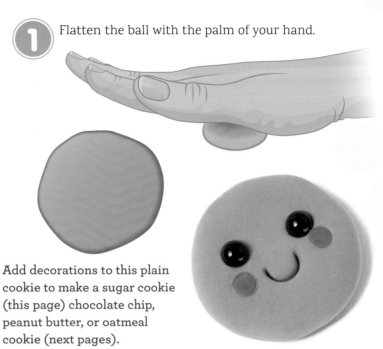

Add decorations to this plain cookie to make a sugar cookie (this page) chocolate chip, peanut butter, or oatmeal cookie (next pages).

Sugar

COOKIE ICING

Make a clay ball this big:

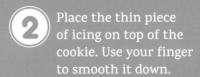

Flatten the clay ball this big:

① To make icing, squish a small ball super flat with your finger. Keep pressing until you have a nice round-ish shape.

② Place the thin piece of icing on top of the cookie. Use your finger to smooth it down.

③ Decorate and glaze the icing only. Add a face (see page 11).

CHOCOLATE CHIP

1 Press the chocolate chips onto the cookie so they stick.

CHOCOLATE CHIPS
Make clay balls this big:

We recommend the size above, but really any teeny tiny clay ball will end up looking like a chocolate chip.

Try a white chocolate-chip cookie.

2 Add a face (see page 11) and paint glaze on the chocolate chips only.

Try a chocolate candy cookie.

Ouch!

USE THIS END OF THE TOOL TO MAKE BITE MARKS:

Press the tool straight down into the clay to make rounded cuts and pull away the clay pieces.

Smooth the cut with your finger or the back side of the tool.

Oatmeal

USE THIS END OF THE TOOL:

Try making an oatmeal raisin cookie!

Gently press the tool into the cookie's surface and all around the cookie's edge to make it look like it's full of oatmeal.

Peanut Butter Blossom

CHOCOLATE CANDY

Make a clay ball this big:

1 To make a chocolate candy, pinch a point on top of the ball.

2 Hold the tip and gently push the chocolate candy against a work surface to flatten the bottom.

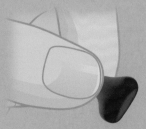

Repinch the tip if needed.

3 Place the chocolate candy in the middle of a cookie. Add a face (see page 11) and paint glaze on the chocolate candy only.

15

Cutout

 **BAKE CHALLENGE**

USE THIS END OF THE TOOL: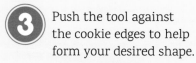

1 Make a cookie and some icing, but don't put them together (yet). See page 13.

2 Press the tool straight down into the clay to make straight cuts and pull away the clay pieces.

3 Push the tool against the cookie edges to help form your desired shape.

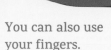

You can also use your fingers.

4 Use Steps 2 and 3 to make the icing the same shape as the cookie. Make it slightly smaller than the cookie.

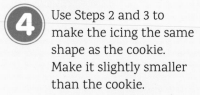

5 Place the icing on the cookie and smooth it down. Decorate and glaze the icing only.

Can you make cutout cookies for your favorite holiday?

SPRING TIME

WARM WISHES

BOO!

Bakery Box

You'll Need:
BOX

The stripes are on the inside of the box.

1 Lay the box flat on a work surface. Fold up the two panels that have slits on them.

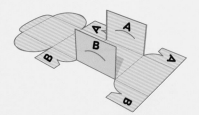

2 Fold up the front panel and tuck side A into slot A and tab B into slot B.

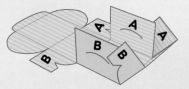

3 Fold up the back panel and tuck side A into slot A and tab B into slot B.

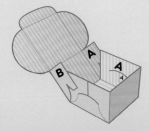

Sweet!

4 When you are ready to close the box, fold down the lid and tuck all tabs inside the box.

TAKE US HOME TODAY!

Try tying up the box with some craft string from home.

17

MacaRon

1 Flatten both cookies and cream with the palm of your hand.

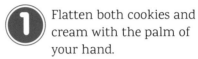

2 Stack the macaron with a cookie on either side of the cream.

MACARON COOKIES

Make two clay balls this big:

CREAM

Make a clay ball this big:

Flatten ALL the clay balls this big:

3 To make the layers stick together gently roll the macaron on its side against the work surface.

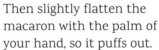

Then slightly flatten the macaron with the palm of your hand, so it puffs out.

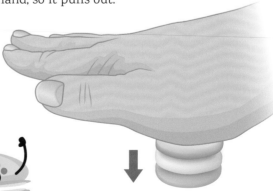

Now make a ruffled edge.

MAKE A RUFFLED EDGE

MACARON RUFFLES

Make two clay balls this big:  → Make two coils this long:

4 Make two coils out of a clay color that matches the cookies. The coils should be long enough to wrap around the cookie's edge.

5 Gently wrap a coil above and below the cream. It should stick to the edges of the cookies.

If the coil is too long, just pinch off the extra clay.

If the coil is too short, gently pull the coil to stretch it longer.

USE THIS END OF THE TOOL:

6 Press the tool into a coil surface and push up to make a ruffle. Do this all the way around the cookie.

7 Turn the cookie upside down and make the ruffle around the other coil.

8 Decorate and add a face (see page 11).

19

CUPCAKE ICING

Make clay balls this big:

CUPCAKE BOTTOM

Make clay balls this big:

Try a colorful clay if you want it to look like a cupcake paper and not cake.

Cupcake

THE BABY OF THE CAKE FAMILY.

1 Roll the cupcake bottom into a cylinder, by rolling it on its side.

2 Sit the cylinder upright, and place the cupcake icing on top of it.

3 Gently press down on the cupcake icing so the cupcake bottom shortens and puffs out. Stop once you like the way it looks.

USE THIS END OF THE TOOL:

4 Lay the cupcake down on your work surface. Use the tool to make a scallop around the bottom of the cupcake icing.

USE THIS END OF THE TOOL:

5 Use the tool to make lines in the cupcake bottom.

Change a cupcake into a mini muffin.

6 Decorate and add a face (see page 11). Sit the cupcake in a paper cup.

21

DAINTY Decorations

CLAY BALL DECORATIONS

Remember, if the clay is too soft to work with, let it rest for a couple minutes, then try the project again. Eventually the clay will firm up and become easier to work with.

PEARLS

Make clay balls this big:

Stick the balls in a line to look like a strand of pearls. Glaze them to add shine.

STRAWBERRIES

Make a clay ball this big:

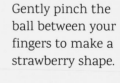

You'll need:
- toothpick from home
- strawberry leaf

Gently pinch the ball between your fingers to make a strawberry shape.

Use a toothpick to poke little dimples all over the strawberry.

Then place the strawberry and add a leaf with glaze.

CLAY COIL DECORATIONS

Let coils set for a few minutes to firm up before you make decorations.

SPRINKLES

Use the straight edge of the tool to cut tiny sprinkles. Let the sprinkles sit for a few minutes so they are more firm and don't stick together. Then paint glaze on top of the pastry wherever you want the sprinkles to stick.

ICING CURLS

On your work surface, make loops with a thin coil. Paint a line of glaze where you want the curls to stick on the treat.

Three curls are perfect for a cupcake. For cakes, make additional icing curls and pinch them together to make an extra-long length of loops.

TWISTY ICING

Paint a line of glaze where you want the rope to stick on the treat.

Make two extra-long coils. Pinch them together at one end, then let the coils sit for a few minutes. After the coils firm up, begin twisting them together.

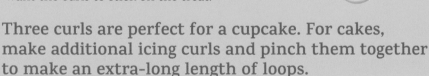

You may need to put a little glaze on the coils after a couple of twists to make it stay together.

Remember, glaze anything you really want to stand out!

TOOTHPICK DECORATIONS

You'll need toothpicks from your kitchen to make these accessories.

 1

Wrap one end of the coil around the toothpick. Press the end onto the remaining coil to make sure it sticks.

Leave some space at the pointy top of the toothpick.

BIRTHDAY CANDLE

Make a clay ball this big:

Make a coil this long:

 2

While holding the tip of the toothpick, start spinning the coil around the toothpick.

The coil won't go the entire length of the toothpick.

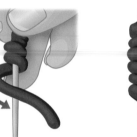

 3

Push the toothpick into the cupcake before you "light" the candle.

4

Make a very small ball and push it on the tip of the toothpick. Pinch the tip to look like a flame.

Add a fun flag or candle to any cake who wants to party!

FUN FLAGS

1 Fold a flag in half and put glaze on the inside of one side.

2 Lay a toothpick along the fold and pinch the flag shut.

PAPER DECORATIONS

Display your cupcakes on a darling doily or in a super-cute cupcake paper.

Push cake toppers right into the clay to make them stick.

Paint glaze where you want to stick on the paper decorations.

Want more cupcake papers?
Look for cupcake papers called Candy Cups at your local craft store.

SECRET RECIPE

Cake Pop

Try this recipe with your decorating skills and things found in your kitchen.

To make the cake pop, push a toothpick into the ball.

Roll a clay ball this big:

You'll need a toothpick.

CINNAMON BUN

A WARM FRIEND THAT MAKES YOU FEEL ALL OOEY-GOOEY INSIDE!

Make a clay ball this big:

1 Roll the cinnamon bun into a cylinder, by rolling it on its side.

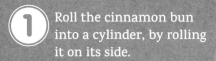

2 Sit the cylinder upright, then gently flatten it down with the palm of your hand until it shortens and puffs out. Stop once you like the way it looks.

Baker's Tip:
If you flattened it too much, roll it on its side again to make it taller. Then repeat Step 2.

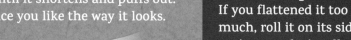

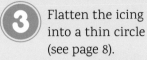
If you want an iced cinnamon bun, follow Steps 3–5. If not, then skip to Step 6.

MAKE DRIPPY ICING

3 Flatten the icing into a thin circle (see page 8).

4 Then gently pull little drips all around the edge.

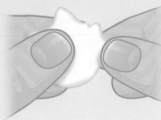

5 Place the drippy icing on top of the cinnamon bun. Use your finger to smooth it down.

MAKE A CINNAMON SWIRL

6 Make a thin coil. Roll one end thinner so that it makes a point.

Make a clay ball this big:

Make a coil this long:

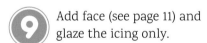

7 Press the pointed end of the coil in the middle of the cinnamon bun so it sticks. Then use your finger to guide the coil into a swirl around the top.

8 Continue the swirl down the side and end underneath the bun. Tear off any extra length coil and smooth the swirl down to make it stick.

9 Add face (see page 11) and glaze the icing only.

27

Slice of Pie

THIS CUTIE PIE
IS FILLED
WITH LOVE.

PIE FILLING

Make a clay
ball this big:

You'll Need:
PIE
FORM

START WITH THE PIE FILLING

1 Flatten the pie filling with the palm of your hand. Stop flattening once the pie form can sit in the middle and have clay showing around all three sides.

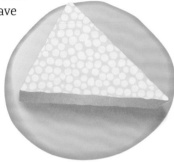

Baker's choice:
You can gently roll the tool over the pie filling if you want it to stretch a little more.

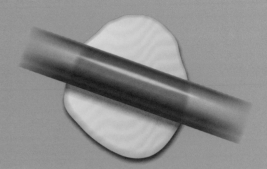

Icing may stick to the roller for the first few rolls. You can lay a piece of wax paper on top of the clay, then roll until the clay starts to flatten.

2 Gently begin to cover the pie form with the pie filling. Fold each side over the form, like you are wrapping a gift.

3 Use your fingers to smooth and work the clay until the form is completely covered and looks smooth on each side.

If any area gets too thick, just pinch off the extra clay.

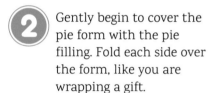

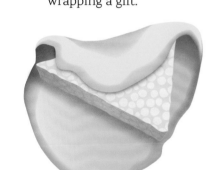

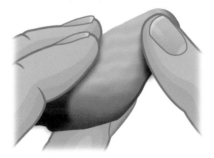

Decide which side of the filling is the best to face up and set it aside for now.

TIME TO ADD THE CRUST.

29

MAKE THE Pie Crust

4 Flatten the pie crust with the palm of your hand. Stop flattening once the pie filling can sit in the middle and have clay showing all around three sides.

Baker's choice:
You can gently roll the tool over the pie filling if you want it to stretch a little more.

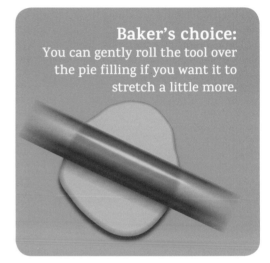

USE THIS END OF THE TOOL:

5 Use the pie filling as a guide and cut along the sides of the filling.

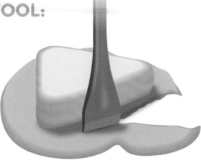

Save the pieces you cut off the sides. You'll need them to finish the edge of the pie crust.

TOP VIEW

STOP!
Don't cut the bottom of the triangle (yet).

6 Gently fold up the longer edge of the pie crust against the filling. The edge will stick up above the pie filling.

7 Tilt the pie slice up. Use the pie filling as a guide and trim the long edge of the crust even with the filling.

8 Sit the pie back down and smooth the sides of the pie crust to the filling. Do this on all sides of the crust until you like the way it looks.

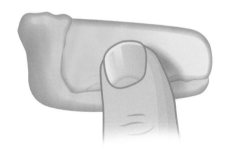

SIDE VIEW

FINISH THE PIE CRUST

9 Roll the clay you cut off the crust into a small ball.

Then roll that scrap ball into a coil.

10 Lay the coil above the top of the pie. Cut the coil to match the width.

Use your finger to smooth the cut edge of the crust to match the other side,

11 Lay the trimmed coil on the edge of the pie on top of the filling.

TURN THE PAGE TO FINISH THE CRUST.

USE THIS END OF THE TOOL:

12 Make a ruffled edge (see page 19). Press the tool into the coil surface and push up to make a ruffle. Do this all the way across the edge of the crust.

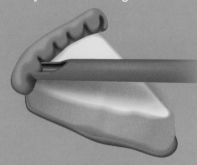

Ruffle both sides if you want.

13 Add a face (see page 11) to the top or side of the pie slice.

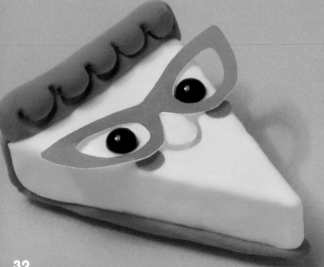

Can you make a fruity dessert?

Use craft materials from home or the craft store.

CHERRY PIE

Add a top crust to any pie with pie crust scraps.

BLUEBERRY PIE

Use beads as tiny berries. You may need glue to make them stick.

STRAWBERRY CHEESECAKE

Try adding drippy icing and some clay strawberries.

À La Mode
(SCOOP OF ICE CREAM)

ICE CREAM SCOOP	Make a clay ball this big:	
RUFFLED EDGE	Make a clay ball this big:	

Make a coil this long for a ruffled edge:

① Hold the ice cream scoop on both sides, then gently tap the ball against your work surface to make a flattened bottom.

② Add a ruffled edge (see page 19) around the entire scoop.

③ Use the tool to add texture to the scoop of ice cream

Use glaze to make the ice cream stick.

Whipped Cream

That was easy as pie!

Make a clay ball this big:

Make a coil this long:

① Make a point on each end of the coil by pinching it.

② Twirl the coil into a pile of whipped cream.

Use glaze to make the whipped cream stick.

Cake

THIS CHEERFUL CHARACTER IS ALWAYS THE LIFE OF THE PARTY.

LARGE CAKE

Make a clay ball this big:

Use the clay roller and roll the ball flat until it's this big:

You'll Need:

LARGE CAKE FORM

HOW TO ROLL
FroSting

Take your time! Rolling frosting for a cake is different than icing a cookie or donut.

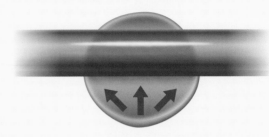

ROLLING TIPS:

- Roll on your work surface and not inside the book. Once the clay starts to look big enough, pick it up and check it against the visual guide.

- Roll the clay roller just to the edge of the frosting. This helps you make a circle.

- If your circle is a little wobbly, use the tool to cut the edges.

USE THIS END OF THE TOOL:

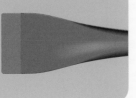

1 Flatten the ball with the palm of your hand. Place the roller in the middle of the frosting and start rolling back and forth, lightly pressing against the clay.

2 Once you almost reach the edge of the frosting, STOP. Pick up the roller and center it on the frosting. Roll again, alternating directions.

3 Keep rolling in different directions until you have an even piece of frosting in a circle-ish shape.

If you need to start over, roll it back into a ball and try again.

Place the cake form in the middle of the frosting, so the clay is showing all around the form.

 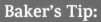 Gently begin to cover the cake form with the frosting. Fold each side over the form, like you are wrapping a gift.

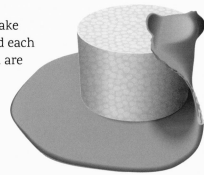

Baker's Tip:
While wrapping, if you find that the frosting is too short to reach the top of the cake form, then gently pull the frosting to stretch it. Then continue wrapping.

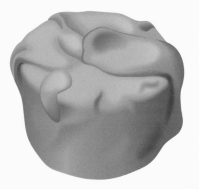

 Continue to wrap. Use your fingers to smooth and work the clay until the form is completely covered.

The top of the cake will look very lumpy. You may also have a few wrinkles on the sides of the cake.

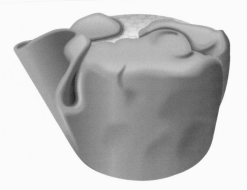

If you get any tears in the frosting while wrapping, just add a piece of flattened clay on top to patch up the hole.

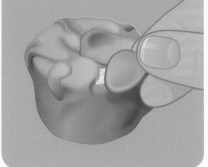

HOW TO SMOOTH FROSTING

7 Gently press the frosting down to the cake form.

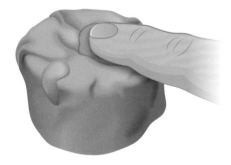

8 Once it looks smoother, start pushing the extra clay toward the edge of the cake with your thumb and pointer finger.

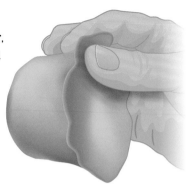

Keep working out all the lumps and bumps until you like the way the frosting looks.

The extra frosting should stick out past the cake form, like this.

USE THIS END OF THE TOOL:

9 Use the cake as a guide and cut along the sides of the extra frosting.

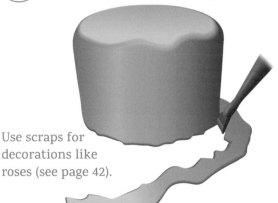

Use scraps for decorations like roses (see page 42).

10 Smooth down any rough cut edges with your finger.

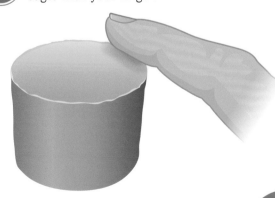

TURN THE PAGE TO FIND MORE SMOOTHING TECHNIQUES AND TO ADD FINSHING TOUCHES.

37

SMOOTHING TIPS

Try any or all of these smoothing techniques until the frosting looks good to you.

With two fingers, roll the cake on its side against your work surface.

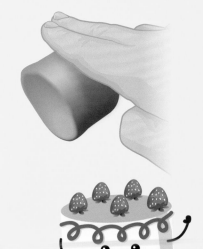

With the palm of your hand, gently press the cake against the work surface to flatten the top and bottom of the cake.

Add a drop of water, then use your finger to rub it into the clay until the surface is smooth.

Don't worry if your frosting isn't perfectly smooth, you can cover some of your cake with decorations.

Decorate the cake as is or turn to pages 44–47 to add more cake layers, then decorate!

Cake Stand

You'll Need:

2 STANDS

CAKE PLATE

1 Slide the stand together in an "X" shape.

2 Fold down all the scallops on the cake plate.

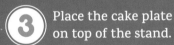

3 Place the cake plate on top of the stand.

There are 4 slots where the stand will fit into the cake plate.

BoWS

DRESS UP YOUR DESSERTS

Make a clay ball this big:

Make a coil this long:

1 Use the roller to flatten the coil into an even ribbon.

2 THE ROLLED RIBBON SHOULD BE ABOUT THIS LONG:

Trim off a scrap of about ½ inch (13 mm) and set it aside for now.

3 Make a loop with the ribbon.

4 Carefully place the ribbon loop on its side with the seam facing toward the left.

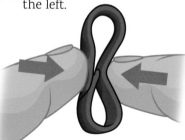

With one finger on each side of the loop, slowly push the middle together.

5 Flip the bow down so the seam is on the bottom.

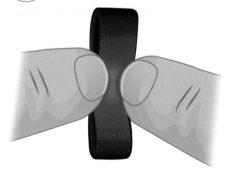

Then with one finger on each side of the bow, lightly squeeze in the middle until it makes dents.

40

6 Take the scrap you cut off the long ribbon in Step 2, and roll that into a skinny coil.

7 Use the roller to flatten the coil into an even, skinny ribbon.

This skinny ribbon should be thinner than the bow.

8 Lay the skinny ribbon over the top of the bow in the middle. Gently push the sides in so they stick to the bow.

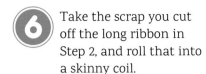

USE THIS SIDE OF THE TOOL:

9 Use the tool to trim off the extra clay. Let the bow rest for several minutes before you handle it.

RIBBON TIPS:

- Using the roller to flatten coils can be a great way to make other trims for decorating.

- The secret to making perfect ribbons is to press evenly when you roll the coils.

Try to make different size bows.

Change the length or thickness of the coil.
The smaller the loop = the smaller the bow.

ADVANCED DECORATING

Can you master this classic cake decoration?

Roses

 ① **Make a clay ball this big:**

Then separate the ball into at least nine tiny balls. Try to make them the same size.

② Use your thumb to flatten each tiny ball to make rose petals.

Flatten ALL the clay balls this big:

ROSE TIPS:

- Odd numbers of petals make the prettiest roses.
- To make smaller roses use fewer petals or start with smaller petal balls.

---

③ Lay the toothpick on the left side of one of the flattened petals.

Roll the petal around the toothpick. Gently pinch at the base of the rose to make it stick to the toothpick.

④ Add the next petal to the side of the center of the rose. Line up the tops.

Continue to do this with each petal, alternating the sides you wrap petals on.

Give a gentle pinch at the base every once in a while to make the petals stick together.

5 Stop once you run out of petals or when you like how full the rose looks.

6 Carefully pull the rose up and off the toothpick. It's easiest to twist the toothpick out while sliding the rose off.

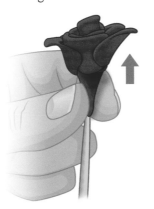

7 Use the tool to cut off the extra clay at the base.

Baker's choice:
For a more natural look, while waiting for the rose to dry, you can gently bend down the edge of the petals with a toothpick.

HOW TO ATTACH ROSES

Add punch-out leaves or try making your own out of green clay.

Usually by the time you are ready to decorate, your cake's frosting is already starting to dry.

1 To add roses, attach fresh tiny balls of clay anywhere you want a rose. Use the same color of the frosting so it doesn't show.

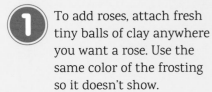

2 Then paint some glaze on top of the extra frosting balls and press the rose into the new clay and glaze.

This works great for one flower or a cluster!

Two-Layer Cake

Make a second layer to add on top of a large cake.

Use the recipe below, but follow the same directions as the Large Cake (see pages 34–38) to make the medium cake. Turn the page to see how to attach the cakes together.

MEDIUM CAKE

Roll a clay ball this big:

Use the roller tool and roll the ball flat until it's this big:

You'll Need:
MEDIUM CAKE FORM

TRiPLe-LaYeR Cake

Make a tiny third layer to add on top of a two-layer cake.

Use the recipe below, but follow the same directions as the Large Cake (see pages 34–38) to make the small cake. Turn the page to see how to attach the cakes together.

SMALL CAKE

Roll a clay ball this big:

Use the roller tool and roll the ball flat until it's this big:

You'll Need:
SMALL CAKE FORM

TURN THE PAGE TO SEE HOW TO ATTACH CAKE LAYERS TOGETHER.

HOW TO ATTACH CAKE LAYERS

If the cake's frosting is still wet, simply stack the layer on top. The wet clay will stick to each other.

If a cake's frosting has started to dry, then paint glaze on top of where you want to stack another smaller cake.

Cake Characters

Baker's choice:
Decide which layer the face will go on.

Remember: Add a face (see page 11) after you have decorated.

Can you make a mini version of your favorite cake?

Use craft materials from home or the craft store.

Find a picture of a cake from a magazine, online, or your own birthday. Try to make a smaller version for the mini bake shop.